a reason for
HOPE

OVERCOMING EARTHLY STRUGGLES
AND LOOKING FORWARD TO HEAVEN

Pastor Mark Jeske

Published by Straight Talk Books
P.O. Box 301, Milwaukee, WI 53201
800.661.3311 · timeofgrace.org

Printed in the United States of America
ISBN: 978-0-9910967-7-0

Introduction

We try so hard to get everything under control. We work so hard to live and stay healthy, save a little money, get along with people, have some peace in the family. We labor at getting a good education, finding the right job and career, finding the right spouse.

Then stuff happens. Nobody can avoid the inevitable breakdowns of life. Because of other people's sins, because of our own sins, because of Satan's relentless attacks, our lives suffer setbacks—job loss, financial loss, illness, disabilities, family breakdown. Death is a stealthy invader of our lives.

We are all starving for love and hope. That's why the gospel message of Jesus is so sweet to our ears. The Word tells us that God's love for us is unconditional, that through Jesus we are loved and forgiven now and forever. His words of grace are new and fresh to us every morning.

The Father promises to be with us in our struggles, to lend his mighty Spirit to give us vision in the darkness, light on our path, clarity of thinking, patience and stamina in our souls, faith in our hearts, friends for the journey, and meaningful work to do. He even promises to make all our hardships work for us and for his loving agenda.

Best of all, we know that at the end of our lives, when death draws near, whether we die abruptly or slowly, the gates of heaven swing open for us, framing the welcoming figure of Jesus our Savior with arms open wide. All the believers who have gone ahead of us are right behind him, waiting to include us in the grand reunion.

I hope you enjoy the three stories in this book. May they give you comfort, hope, and joy for the journey.

Pastor Mark Jeske

Holy Spirit,

I need your help, and I need it now. I'm tired. So many things I've tried to control just keep breaking down. So many things I want just keep dancing out of my reach. So many people I counted on have let me down.

And it's not just other people's fault. I'm embarrassed at how weak my faith is sometimes and how my selfish and careless actions must disappoint you. How desperately I need my Savior's forgiveness; how glad I am that his mercy is fresh and new every morning.

Spirit, keep me looking forward, not backward. Keep me looking up at Jesus, not down at my sinful feet. Keep me optimistic, not brooding on lost money or lost opportunities. Help me believe more strongly than ever that any day in heaven will be better than my best day on earth, and use me to share faith and hope with the people in my life.

It's through Jesus that I pray, Amen.

A Better World Is Coming

Take a moment right now and check your stress level. Is your life purring along just fine? Is the ride a little bumpy right now? Are you undergoing major turbulence? Or is your personal needle in the red zone?

I had a couple of major anxiety moments like that myself this week. I want you to know that whether your week was crummy or okay or great, Jesus was there with you. I want you also to know that even when the needle in your life is lingering in the red zone of stress, even when you're burying the needle at the upper end, Jesus is there too. Even when it looks like your life is coming apart, the Lord has an answer for absolutely everything.

His short-term answer is to provide enough daily resources to manage. His ultimate answer is to come back to make a world way better than the one you're living in.

Sooner or later you are going to leave this world. Either one of two things is going to happen: you are going to die, or judgment day is going to come first. The ordinary pace of life—the sun rises, we move around; the sun sets, we go to bed and sleep—that rhythm, which seems like it will never change, will abruptly change. I want you to know that the Lord says, "I can do a whole lot better than the life you're living right now. I want you to hang on because I'm coming to bring you into my new world."

The Father who loves you—your Creator and Sustainer—knows your troubles and stress and cares deeply about what's happening in your life. Perhaps you had a pretty good week. But sooner or later bad stuff is going to come slamming into you that will make you sick of this place, and I want you to know that God is neither silent nor apathetic nor helpless. In fact, he says that his answer to our pain was to send Jesus, his Son, to maximum pain.

Even when it looks like your life is coming apart, the Lord has an answer for absolutely everything.

The prophet Isaiah, in the sweep of 66 chapters and seven centuries before these things actually happened, prophesied the complete ministry of Jesus. His birth, his life, his ministry, his suffering, his death, and his triumphant resurrection are all told in prophetic form in the chapters preceding what we are going to concentrate on here.

The Lord's answer to your suffering is this: "I'm going to do some spot repairs to help you get through this life, but my ultimate answer is to start over. I am going to create a new heaven and a new earth. Everything will be new. And those who trust and believe in the Lord Jesus Christ as their Savior will come to live with me."

In the verses right before Isaiah 65:17, Isaiah has a few things to say to the people who don't believe what he's telling them. It's not good news. Speaking for the Lord he says, **"My servants will eat, but you will go hungry"** (verse 13), meaning that Jesus is the answer to every basic human need. When you're with him, your life will be full and your eternity will be spectacular. Without him **"you will go hungry; my servants will drink, but you will go thirsty; my servants will rejoice, but you will be put to shame. My servants will sing out of the joy of their hearts, but you will cry out from anguish of heart"** (verses 13,14). So a great shaking out is coming, when the Lord is going to do some mighty separating. These issues are issues of life and death, and I want you to hear clearly the dreadful fate that awaits those who reject God's rescue plan. But I'd like to invite you to experience the incredible promises that the Lord designed for what is coming for the believers.

In verse 17 there is something to hang on to

when the needle in your life goes into the red or when someone you love has the needle buried in the red. Here are some words of hope that will sustain you and me in anything: **"Behold** (that's God's way of saying, "Listen! Pay attention!"), **I will create new heavens and a new earth."** The new world will be better than the one you're living in now. In the present world, you and I, with our five senses, cannot perceive God directly. Only through our faith can we perceive that God is here. We can't touch God, we can't taste God, we can't smell God, we can't see God, and we can't hear God directly. But the Lord tells us through his Word, the Bible, that he will make a new heaven and a new earth.

Now here come seven spectacular promises of how the new world is going to be better than the old:

First: **"The former things will not be remembered, nor will they come to mind. But be glad and rejoice forever in what I will create"** (verses 17,18). One of the things that gives me pain today is dragging around memories of yesterday's pain. Isn't that sad? People who have made me sad *once* in the past have the power to make me sad *every time* I think back on them. Is this just my problem, or do you drag around a lot of pain in your memories too? The divorce hurt the year it happened, and it keeps hurting. The abuse hurt when you were in middle school, and remembering it still hurts today. The bullying hurt once, and it still hurts to think about it.

Sometimes I wish my brain was like a computer. I could do a pain scan of all the files in my memories, and I could hit the delete button all afternoon, selectively taking out all the "hurting" stuff. **The former things will not be remembered.** God means that the former *bad* things, the painful things, will not be remembered. So your past will lose its power to torment and hurt you. This doesn't mean that in heaven you will experience total amnesia with everything about your identity, history, and relationships wiped out. God promises that he will do a selective memory delete, and you are not going to be hurt anymore from the things that are hurting you now.

Second: Look at the second half of verse 19. Here's a promise: **"The sound of weeping and of crying will be heard in it no more."** I don't like that stuff in my life, and I don't like it when I see you weeping and crying; that hurts my heart too. God guarantees you and me an existence in which we will no longer need to cry. Not only will your hurting memories be removed, but you won't be hurt again. Your tear ducts will return to their originally designed use, which is lubricating the eyeball and moistening up with pride or joy.

Here's God's *third* promise: **"Never again will there be in it an infant who lives but a few days, or an old man who does not live out his years; he who dies at a hundred will be thought a mere youth; he who fails to reach a hundred will be considered accursed"** (verse 20). This sounds as if there is going to be death in heaven, but it's sort of God's little joke. There is no death in the new heaven and the new earth. You will all hit one hundred and then just keep going.

This third promise is just saying that one of the worst parts of living in the world that you and I have to live in now is premature death. In our earthly lives, if somebody makes it to one hundred, people say he or she lived a full life. But premature death is a different story. I can't imagine a greater hurt than to hold the corpse of your child in your arms and wish you could do something to bring that child back to life. The child was stolen away from you by death.

Premature death is maybe one of the worst hurts we have to endure. Many people do not live to be one hundred. They're chopped down by violence,

Your past will lose its power to torment and hurt you.

they get into accidents, they get sick, and there are many other ways that death stalks us and cuts us down. God says that in the new world none of that will ever happen again. Never again will there be an infant who lives but a few days.

Look at verses 21 and 22 for promise number *four:* **"They will build houses and dwell in them; they will plant vineyards and eat their fruit. No longer will they build houses and others live in them, or plant and others eat."** In other words, there will be no injustice in heaven. The strong won't tyrannize and dominate the weak. The powerful won't oppress the powerless. People won't pour out their labor only to increase the wealth of someone else and after a lifetime of work end up with nothing. How do you think it felt to be a slave working on a plantation, building a big house for the master? The master got the big house, and the slave spent his days in a little hut in the back. God says your labor in heaven will not be stolen from you by unjust practices and cruel tyranny. You will build houses, and *you* will live in them. You will plant vineyards, and *you* will eat what you grow. The point is that there will be an end to the injustices of labor in which the many are ripped off by the oppression and greed of a few.

Fifth: **"For as the days of a tree, so will be the days of my people"** (verse 22). There are some trees that have hundreds of rings in their stumps. Now this is not to say that you're going to last a little bit longer than you normally would, but the point is that we human beings are outlasted on this earth by plants—that's how fragile we are. Your existence is not going to be chopped short, but you are going to go even beyond the trees, and there'll be lots of "rings" in you. **"My chosen ones will long enjoy the works of their hands. They will not toil in vain or bear children doomed to misfortune"** (verses 22,23). In this life some people are in such a deep hole, they struggle so bad that, essentially, their children are cursed to be stuck in that same hole. One of the things that I will rejoice in when I get to heaven is that I don't have to push my little chicks out of the nest into a world as full of violence and drugs, cruelty and greed, and oppression and violence as is present in this world.

Here's another good thing, promise number *six*: **"Before they call I will answer; while they are still speaking I will hear"** (verse 24). In heaven God will anticipate your communications and requests even before you say them. This is a little poetic suggestion to the fact that God will not be seen as distant. He'll be right there. In fact, the book of Revelation says you won't even need to have a sun in the sky in heaven because the Lamb will be at the center and he will be the light.

You will always be in the presence of God. You

and I will enjoy what now we have to strain to imagine. When we live in the new heaven and the new earth that God is going to make, we will have direct interaction with him. In fact, he will answer our requests before we even get the thoughts out of our mouths. You will not only live forever. You will be cared for forever.

There is one *last* blessing listed in these verses: **"The wolf and the lamb will feed together, and the lion will eat straw like the ox"** (verse 25). Doesn't that seem a little weird to you? What do you know about wolves and lambs? If I were a lamb, I sure wouldn't be anywhere near a wolf. But God says in the world in which he is going to create, the smaller and weaker will not need to fear those who are unlike them or bigger or stronger. For there will be no violence; there will be no cruelty and oppression. There will be no more of this preying on the weak. God uses animal metaphors, but his real point is that lamblike people will no longer have to be afraid of other people.

Women can get really excited about this promise. One of the sad and bitter features of living in our world

When we live in the new heaven and the new earth that God is going to make, we will have direct interaction with him.

is that if you're female, you are vulnerable and attract attention that often you do not want. There are many, many places a female does not feel safe. And that level of fear is always there, isn't it? You may feel like a lamb walking around this world, in a place full of wolves, but I've got some news for you, and I speak especially to all the females. No "wolf" is ever going to mess with you again when you are living in the new heaven and the new earth. **"They will neither harm nor destroy on all my holy mountain"** (verse 25). The reason for that is a little clue right in verse 25: **"The lion will eat straw like the ox."** In other words, see those vicious teeth that lions use to rip the flesh off their prey? God might just turn them into cud chewers. Lions will munch on grass. Isn't that a concept?

This is a metaphor, of course. The point is that all the things that make some people threats to others will be taken away by God. Weapons, for instance. There will be no need for weapons when every last person in heaven is your friend. You will never fear another human being.

But look what the meal of the serpent will be. Notice he doesn't talk about snakes in general but in particular: **"Dust will be the serpent's food,"** and that's a little reminder why living in heaven is going to be so much fun. The serpent isn't going to be there anymore. Even in the Garden of Eden, as beautiful and perfect as that place was, evil slithered. Evil was looking for a chance to strike. Here is the ultimate: In heaven you and I will be freed from the temptation, the presence, and the lies of Satan, from his evil assaults for ever and ever. Satan will not be the king of hell. He will be its most notorious prisoner and suffer for what he has done. He will truly eat dust.

"They will neither harm nor destroy on all my holy mountain." Maybe your life is okay right at this moment, but you're going to need to know where this passage in Isaiah is. So put a note in the front of your Bible: *"In times of danger, read Isaiah 65:17–25."*

Somebody you encounter in the next month is going to have his or her needle buried in the red zone. Now you're armed and dangerous because you can pass on to people that there is hope so strong that it is stronger than any misery that

In times of danger, read Isaiah 65:17–25.

anyone is undergoing right at this moment. I want you to know that these wonderful things have been guaranteed to you by the Lord himself, who loves you. Come soon, Lord Jesus!

Dear Lord Jesus,

I want to be brave in adversity. I try to be brave. But you know my heart. You know how foggy my vision is, how short my sight, how materialistic I get, how fearful I become. All around me I see only death—help me see life in the Easter stories from your wonderful Word.

Have patience with me when I doubt. Lift my eyes to your cross to gain absolute confidence of my forgiveness and your Father's favor. Direct my eyes to your empty tomb to see there the promise of my own resurrection. Your path to glory lay through hardship and suffering first, and so does mine.

Lord Jesus, give me faith as I wait for sight; give me hope as I wait for glory. It is in your name that I pray, Amen.

Guaranteed: Life After Death

I saw a T-shirt once that read, "Life is short; eat more chocolate." Is that how you feel? I don't mean, "Do you like chocolate?" Everybody likes chocolate. What I mean is, "Do you feel the pressure to go, go, go, to pack as many experiences in as you can because life's slipping away from you?"

I'd like to tell you the greatest of all stories in the Bible. It's the resurrection of Jesus, which takes all the pressure off of us because it opens up an eternity of time. The part I want to focus on is only two paragraphs from John chapter 20. It shows us how some doubters of Jesus' rising were made confident, doubters just like you and me because we too have fear and act sometimes as though the resurrection of Christ didn't happen. We act as though *our* resurrection isn't really going to happen either, and we get that panic: "Got to do it now! Hurry, hurry; time is slipping away. Soon, game over!"

John chapter 20 is the Sunday story following a very ugly Friday, the Friday on which Jesus suffered, died, and was buried. It seemed like a total defeat to his followers. And I think I know why they didn't believe—they were looking at the evidence of their eyes. They saw a man really dead, a man who was killed like a criminal.

On the Saturday after that horrible Friday, Jesus left it all behind and went in spirit to hell to proclaim his victory. But while he was doing a lap in the enemy's capital, *he allowed his friends to have a miserable day*! And you get that, don't you? You've also had days when you could not see or perceive Easter. You've had days that look like total misery and defeat: maybe a day when you're in deep debt and then get fired and have no income to handle your debts, or a day when someone you love gets a cancer diagnosis.

Some of you have laid dear friends and loved ones to rest, and yet *you* aren't at rest. Maybe you've been dragging yourself around with chronic pain. Some of you have disabilities that really make your life hard. Some of you have been dumped and abandoned by people you thought were trustworthy, and now you're so fearful that you don't know if you can trust anybody again. Some of you have been ripped off financially by the greed or stupidity of somebody else, or perhaps by your own ignorance or carelessness.

> *You've also had days when you could not see or perceive Easter.*

You don't see Easter all the time, and your heart is heavy. Just like yours, the hearts of Jesus' friends were heavy. But then, at the crack of dawn on Sunday, God shook the earth and knocked down the guards. An angel simply rolled the gravestone away, and Jesus left his clothes neatly folded. He made his bed, which is really cool, I think, to show that it was done intentionally. Everything was neatly folded; a little clue for the doubters. He left his grave clothes behind and walked out of his empty tomb.

That's when the first visitor, Mary Magdalene, came to finish the job that she couldn't trust the men to do. Jesus had not merely been anointed and prepared for burial by Joseph of Arimathea and Nicodemus; they also wound him in linen. And Mary Magdalene maybe *wanted* to perform this act of service now that the game was over. Maybe she thought: "Now that all is lost, this will help bring closure to my dead hopes." Now that Jesus was dead, it seemed like everything he was bringing about was now over, game over. And with the heaviest of hearts, she dragged her steps to perform the last rites of her personal anointing on the dead body.

Mary **"saw that the stone had been removed from the entrance. So she came running to Simon Peter and the other disciple, the one Jesus loved** [i.e., John]" (John 20:1,2).

"They have taken the Lord out of the tomb," she said (verse 2). She didn't say, "He arose as he said." She meant, "Grave robbers beat us to it. They've already been here." You know, we don't have so much grave robbing today. It's severely penalized and nobody buries anything worth anything in a grave anymore. But back in the day when there were fantasies about taking some wealth with you into the afterlife, people would sometimes be buried with expensive jewelry or gold or gems and there was a terrible business in grave robbing.

"We don't know where they have put him!" So she already had these sick, sad doubts cooking in her head. **"So Peter and the other disciple started for the tomb. Both were running, but the other disciple outran Peter and reached the tomb first. He bent over,"** saw the **"strips of linen lying there,"** but he didn't go in. Then Peter finally caught up: **"Simon Peter, who was behind him, arrived and went into the tomb. He saw the strips of linen lying there, as well as the burial cloth that had been around Jesus' head. The cloth was folded up by itself, separate from the linen. Finally the other disciple, who had reached the tomb first, also went inside. He saw and believed"** (John 20:3-8). John believed first, but

"they," including John, **"still did not understand from Scripture that Jesus *had* to rise from the dead"** (verse 9). He had said he would; it was the plan. It was the integral part of the entire rescue operation that Jesus led in person.

Yet they still had a horrible, ugly day. In fact, it wasn't until nighttime when Jesus finally appeared to them all that it looked like some of their doubts were transformed into faith. I want to think with you for just a few minutes about this business of doubting. I know why they doubted; I would have too! In fact, I still have my doubts. Sometimes I say I believe, but I act like I don't. I know why they didn't. Their eyes were the evidence they thought they could rely on. God's promises to us are invisible much of the time and only slowly do we begin to see the new reality. Scripture says our lives are hidden in Christ. We so much want to live in the material world that it's hard for us to imagine there's a much greater, vaster world of spirit outside of the material world. And we get caught up in the Now because it's addictive, because it's immediate, and because the devil owns the short term.

The devil gets all of the pleasures, the addictive pleasures, at his disposal to get your attention now. Anger feels good for the first five seconds, doesn't it? Long-term anger destroys. Committing adultery has excitement at the front end, but only damage, guilt, and a feeling of dirt and self-hatred in the long run. Using drugs recreationally gives you a short-term buzz of feeling like it's all okay or "I don't feel that pain anymore," but it leaves you addicted and depressed and craving an ever bigger pop.

We could list another 20 behaviors where the devil always seems to own the short term, and when we talk about the resurrection of Christ, we are only seeing with our eyes that nothing seems to have happened. We've

God's promises to us are invisible much of the time and only slowly do we begin to see the new reality.

been to so many funerals, and death seems final— game over! We all know death is chasing us like a reaper, and so that gives us the creeps; gives us sadness when we think about it or inspires us to pretend that it isn't going to happen. We try to distract ourselves to push off those stressful thoughts.

Another reason is that unbelief and doubt are our natural state. Belief in the words of God is *learned* behavior; it has to be *given* to us. Half the time we don't *really* believe the words of God. Jesus had told his disciples over and over and had repeatedly demonstrated that the One who would be put to death for the sins of the world would rise again. Jesus told his disciples on at least a half dozen different occasions, "I will be buried and in three days rise again." They didn't believe it at the time, and when crunch time came, they didn't believe it then either. In fact, some of them, Mr. Doubting Thomas, for example, couldn't even believe it *when they saw Jesus right in front of them*! Jesus had to say, "Touch me." He had to do an eating demonstration to show that he could eat food like the real human being that he is.

Another thing is that doubt is contagious. When someone else writes the script, we tend to listen to it. If other people say, "I'm scared to die," then we're scared. If somebody else says, "I'm afraid"

> We allow other doubters to frame the issues and inspire us to doubt even more.

or "Life is so short. Get chocolate fast; must eat chocolate now," then we get ramped up in that too. "Hurry, hurry, hurry! Game's almost over. Faster, faster! Pack it in. Get that trip to Europe. Go down south; go to Mexico like you've always wanted. Hurry, get to the bucket list faster, faster, faster before the buzzer goes off because we don't know how long we have." And the devil says,

"Quick! Cheat! You've got a right to it! Go for it!" We allow other doubters to frame the issues and inspire us to doubt even more.

I'm here to tell you that I believe in the resurrection of the body. We say that we believe it, but today is the day to get really, really serious about saying, "I believe in the resurrection of the body." Not to say your spirit won't be resurrected as well. That will go first, actually. But you not only will be raised in spirit immediately, you will be raised someday in body, and in your flesh you will see your Savior.

The resurrection of the body of Christ is everything for you and for me.

Let God's Word tell you the truth that Jesus Christ rose physically out of his grave and in spirit and body met and loved and resumed his relationship with his disciples—never again to die. It wasn't game over. It's a new game, endless game, immortal game, everlasting game.

The resurrection of the body of Christ is *everything* for you and for me. It guarantees that we don't have to panic or think that when death comes it takes things away from us permanently.

We are all optimists because the resurrection of Christ guarantees the forgiveness of our sins. It shows the Father's approval of everything that went before, and it shows that Jesus' blood sacrifice was enough. The blood of God is big enough to wash all of us.

The resurrection of Christ guarantees *your* resurrection. The immortality of Christ guarantees *your* immortality. We can enjoy our lives right now because all the pressure is off! There is no such thing as a disaster because God even turns the hard things in our lives into blessings to make us more useful. We are just working out right now; this is like spring training, and all the stuff we go through—even the stress we go through—is all being hooked and used together just to make us better and more useful, not only now but in eternity. That means you and I are brokers and merchants and reflectors of God's love, and we don't have to sell it because we can *give* it away. We are the sales force; we are the marketing reps for the most amazing message, the most amazing product, in human history.

> We can enjoy our lives right now because all the pressure is off!

You and I are able to let people know that they are loved unconditionally by God, that they have all been redeemed by his blood that was shed for them, and that death itself is nothing. It's not even an enemy anymore; it's merely a gateway to a splendid new life of immortality. You and I can share also the power of the Holy Spirit to believe it, to turn our doubts into confidence, turn our pessimism into optimism, turn our bitterness into joy, and turn our backward look into a look into the windshield.

This is Jesus' gift to you. It is good news for God's people, now and always. Christ is risen!

Dear heavenly Father,

Why do the fading and cheap things of this world have such a grip on my heart and imagination? Send your Spirit to help me win the battle against materialism. My appetites and cravings shout "Here!" and "Now!" Your Word softly breathes "There." "Then."

Heaven will be so much better than anything this world can offer. Please help me listen more closely to your phenomenal promises about the new life that you will create for me—joy, peace, and absolute security. No more Satan, no more sickness, sin, or dying.

What a pleasure it will be to feel great physically, to love others and start liking myself again, to give myself wholeheartedly to worshiping you. Help me prize the forgiving gospel of Christ as my greatest treasure in this life, so that I can enjoy the great feast with you and all the saints in the next.

It's in Jesus' name that I pray, Amen.

What Will Heaven Be Like?

Think about going on a trip to a place you haven't been before. You have to arrange some kind of lodging, and you're not sure what's available in that town. What do you do? Maybe you'll talk to some friends. Perhaps they've got some information or brochures saved from their last trip to show you. Or maybe you'll talk to a travel agent who will give you a stack of stuff you can look at to imagine what the hotels and attractions are like. As you look, you know they're just pictures, but doing this helps you imagine what life is going to be like in that other place. Or perhaps you'll get on your computer to look up the website and take a virtual tour. It isn't real, but it helps you imagine what that place is like.

I went through this process when I had to go to New Mexico for a conference and had to decide where to stay for two days. I could pick the hotel that looked the nicest on the basis of the pictures and information on the brochures and the websites.

I would like to share with you the travel brochure for heaven. I haven't been there, but I've got the brochure and the website. We can take a virtual tour of heaven. God wants you to know what lies ahead. He has not left you clueless, backing you into the future like a train in reverse going down the tracks, caboose first. I know sometimes it seems like that. Sometimes I feel like I'm tied to the back of a train, racing down the tracks, and all I see is the view behind me. I can see the past a lot more clearly than I can see the future. I'm sure you know the feeling. But God wants you to know that where you're headed, you don't have to be scared. Heaven is far better than you can imagine.

God wants you to peek ahead at what the last chapter of your life will be like. You don't know what's going to be in all the intermediate chapters; those have not been written yet. God can see them, but he's not telling you what details lie ahead in your life. He does, however, let you peek ahead to the transition because he does not want you to be afraid. He wants you to be confident.

Now, most people have a totally messed up idea of what heaven really is. We humans sling the word *heaven* around in totally inappropriate ways, much as we do the word *hell*. What happens is that we cheapen and garble those two words. When we hear people use the word *hell* in their daily lives, it has nothing to do with the real hell. People use it as an exclamation point in their talk to make others think they're big or that they're grown up. They use it to intensify the things they are saying because they're afraid that they are weak. It's the way a little boy tries to make himself seem like a big boy. Sometimes boys with big bodies talk like that to make themselves seem bigger. Doesn't work, does it!

In the same way, we use the word *heaven* in totally inappropriate ways that make people miss the real point of what heaven is like. People say, "That dessert with triple-rich chocolate fudge was super. Man, I was in heaven." Well, the real heaven is far better than chocolate! You might hear some young woman say, "Oh, I finally got a date with this guy, and it was

Heaven is far better than you can imagine.

heavenly. I was in heaven last night!" Well, sorry. It's too bad your horizons are so low, for God can do far better than that guy. And another person might say, "You know what heaven would be for me? Going to my favorite mall with a credit card that isn't maxed out." C'mon—God can leave that image in the dust. For proof, let's look at God's website. You can find it in Revelation chapter 22. Open to it. Let's take the virtual tour of heaven.

The first two chapters of Genesis tell us how God created the world and the human race. Then the third chapter tells how low we sank. It tells of a rebellion in a garden—a beautiful place God had created for enjoyment that became a place of curse and pain because of Adam's and Eve's sins. And we are children of those first two sinners. We have been born into that rebellion, stuck with a curse that not only brings us sickness, sadness, and death but also rams us straight to hell.

But Jesus has put up a roadblock. He loves us so much that he put his life on the line so we can live in his house. He wants us to see what he's preparing for the people who trust and believe in his free forgiveness and salvation.

Let's look at the first couple of paragraphs in Revelation chapter 22 to see what heaven is really like. Even though we're not there yet, we can take the virtual tour and get a sense of how tremendous it's going to be.

John wrote the words of Revelation as an old man. He was in his 90s and knew that any day might be his last. But God let him take some peeks at what was coming.

The first thing to notice is that all death will be replaced with life. Look at verses 1 and 2: **"The angel showed me the river of the water of life, as clear as crystal."** No pollution, no muddiness, no impurities, no mercury, no heavy metals, no sewage backup in this water. The Lord's purification plant is far superior to that of any earthly city. Why? It's **"flowing from the throne of God and of the Lamb down the middle of the**

great street of the city." Heaven is a beautiful, grand boulevard flowing out from the throne of God.

Now, whether or not there are going to be actual rivers flowing from the throne of God or whether God is going to need a chair to sit on in heaven is not really important. Some of these details may actually come true, or they may be symbols or pictures of a greater reality. But the point is, in one way or

All death will be replaced with life.

another, all of us who have been cursed with death and are slowly falling apart every day are going to get better. All of us who are mortal, who have to watch ourselves slowly age and shrivel, are going to become immortal. Will we actually take sips of this wonderful healing water or is this just a figure of speech for God touching us with life? It doesn't really matter, does it? Whatever God has planned, it will be perfect.

But right now, death's doing a number on each one of us. We try so hard to hold on to people or to freeze our own lives, but it's like we're strapped to aging machines that rocket us into the grave. I don't mean to be a downer or sound like I'm whining, but let's be honest—we're dying. We try hard to put off what we can't stop. Ladies go to the beauty shop for a few repairs, hoping to delay the inevitable for a little while. Guys buy clothes in styles that produce a slimming effect where they're not slim and provide a little padding to make shoulders where there aren't any. Gravity and time are taking over, whether we like it or not. We work out to stay in shape, but we just cannot stop the aging process. It's chasing us, and it's going to catch us all.

But God has the answer for us, for all of us— soul, spirit, and body. Some people think of heaven as a place where we're going to float around in the clouds, wear a sheet, and play a harp. They think heaven is going to be eight million, zillion years of choir practice. I saw a *Far Side* cartoon where a guy was sitting on a cloud with another guy on a cloud next to him. The first guy says that he's glad not to be in hell. Then he sees the other guy doing nothing and says, "I should've brought a magazine." Will heaven be boring? Not on your life!

You're going to be you in heaven. You're going to be put back together into your ideal state because heaven throbs with life. There's a river full of life that's going to make you well. Verse 2 says, **"On each side of the river stood the tree of life."** You remember the tree of life—the one that God didn't want Adam and Eve to eat from in their sinful state. God kicked them out of the Garden of Eden and put an angel holding a flaming sword in front of the gate so that they couldn't eat from the tree of life and be stuck in their broken state forever. When you're healed and fixed in heaven, you'll love eating fruit from that tree because God will have locked you into eternal life, into immortality, and you'll be well.

All the things that are wrong, broken, or missing from your physical life right now will be restored to you. You're not going to be brought back to life in exactly the same state at which you died. People who fell overboard and were devoured by fish are not going to be missing limbs. People who died at grand old ages after suffering from years of physical debilitation and loss of mental sharpness are not going to be brought back like they were at the moment they died. Children who died in their infancy are not going to need everlasting diaper changes. We will become the ideal of whom God designed us to be. Man, if you think joining the army will help you be all that you can be, imagine what God is going to do to make you all that you can be. Remember, he's the God of limitless power and love. He will make you realize

You're going to be put back together into your ideal state because heaven throbs with life.

your full potential.

Heaven's going to be a place of interesting experiences where we will continue to learn and grow, to enjoy each other, and to enjoy God without fear. **"The leaves of the tree are for the healing of the nations"** (verse 2). We'll be healed. Maybe your life seems good right now: you've got chocolate, a really decent boyfriend or girlfriend, and a credit card for your favorite store at the mall. But is it really that good? Even while you're eating or shopping or enjoying someone else's company, troops are gathering for another fight or somebody in your neighborhood is going down or a relationship is tearing apart or another sniper is planning his moves. Life can be sad and scary. Even as we're talking about the grand things of heaven, there are clans, races, and tribes of people eager to cut each other off. Why? Because people are disconnected from God and are not letting God's love and ways fill their hearts.

Isn't it going to be sweet to live in a world where you don't have to be afraid of anybody else ever again? Isn't it going to be wonderful not to have to deadbolt the front doors where you live? Won't it be nice to never again see car windows smashed out by vandals? Wouldn't you like to live where no one intimidates or hates you? A place where respect replaces racism and kindness cancels out all insults and abuse? Won't it be nice to live where home is a place of peace instead of a place of bitter arguments, ancient grudges, and sinful hostilities? Won't that be sweet? That's heaven. Jesus is there. He makes it sweet.

Heaven is a place of healing where people will be healed in the way they deal with one another. Heaven is a place where we can enjoy our "differentness" without letting Satan use it as a wedge to rip us apart and make us miserable. I want to live in that place; I want to go there. I see little glimmers of it now, but we aren't there yet, are we?

The people around me are of different races and backgrounds. Sometimes we look at each other's potential and what each of us can add instead of letting the differences of age, income, social rank, class, race, skin color, dress, hairstyle, monetary worth, and place of residence become wedge issues to drive us apart. Once in a while we get glimmers of the love that becomes possible through our Lord Jesus. It flickers and cheers us up, but then it goes away, and anger and resentment return. I would like to live in a place where there's love going on all the time. Wouldn't you?

The thing I'm most excited about is getting fixed and healed in heaven. Sometimes I don't like myself very much because I can be such a jerk. I will be glad when I am no longer going to hurt anybody else with my words or actions. I bet you'd like to live in that world too. **"Healing of the nations"** sounds wonderful, doesn't it!

Verse 3 goes on, **"No longer will there be any curse."** We're living under the curse of sin. We rebelled, and God is angry. Why do people die? Do people die of cancer because no cure has yet been found? Suppose that tomorrow someone unlocks the riddle of cancer cells; then we'd die of something else. Okay, suppose cancer gets cured, and the average life expectancy goes from 78 to 79 or 80, and then you die. But you still die. But when there's no curse, it means that the angry hand of God no longer will rest upon a rebellious humanity. It means that our relationship with God will be sweet all the time. No more fear, no more guilt, no more running away from the Garden, no more sin, and no more shame. They'll be gone, and we will be face-to-face with God.

It means that our relationship with God will be sweet all the time.

Right now it can seem like God is distant—that in some ways God has withdrawn himself from us. Many people think there either is no God or that the God out there is impersonal. But through the Word, God reveals that he is a loving, caring God. In heaven his relationship with us will be complete. Think of how much you enjoy Thanksgiving at Grandma's house. Heaven is the ultimate Thanksgiving, Christmas, and Easter all rolled into one.

Verse 3 goes on, **"No longer will there be any curse. The throne of God and of the Lamb will be in the city."** The Savior will be visible so we can interact on a personal basis. Jesus became incarnate not only to have a body to be born with and to live in perfectly for you and for me. He took on human flesh not only to bear our sin and bring our rescue. He was a physical person not only to have a lap for little kids to sit on so he could hug them and demonstrate God's love. He had flesh not only to have something for his enemies to whip, beat, and crown with thorns. He had a body not only to be nailed on that ugly cross and left to hang until dead. And he had a body not only to rise from the dead and demonstrate, as a little test run, what your resurrection is going to look like. Jesus also took his body with him! Yes, he ascended into heaven bodily.

Now in case you missed that, I'm going to rewind that last thought and lay it on you again because it is significant. *He took his body*—his human body, his real body with his lungs, heart, feet, fingernails, and hair—with him to heaven.

And he's keeping it.

What does that tell you about how serious Jesus is about being the bridge between humanity and God? If it were your job to rescue the fish in your fish tank and the only way you could do that was by becoming a fish yourself to communicate with them and live with them for 33 years, you might conceivably do it if you loved your fish enough to keep them from dying. But if I had been a fish for 33 years, I would have then been so glad to ditch the fins and the gills and get my regular self back. I would do the dirty job, be done with it, and then leave the fish alone.

But Jesus stayed human to become accessible to us. In heaven we can hug him when we see him. We might have to stand in line for a little while, for I'm assuming there's going to be a fair crowd around him. But hey, what's the rush? We have forever. Jesus will be close, and we can touch him. He'll stay a person.

Verse 3 continues, **"The throne of God and the Lamb will be in the city, and his servants will serve him."** That's us. We'll rejoice to be God's servants who are finally free from sin and able to find the joy of getting our minds in tune with his mind and will. And it's going to be fun! We're going to be set free to serve.

Verse 4 tells us that we'll **"see his face."** See

God's face! In the Old Testament times when God would stoop close enough to give people a chance to see him in action, he would never let them get too close. Not even Moses, the one God called his friend, was allowed to see God's face. God told Moses to tuck himself into a cleft in the rocks and then God would let him see the afterglow of his glory as he went by. It's as though God said, "Moses, I don't want to fry you, so I won't let you see me. Nobody

In heaven there will be no doubt that you are a child of God.

can see my face and live." But in heaven we will see God's face and live. Why? Because our sins will be gone. The holiness that glows from him, the fire and the glow, will not burn us any longer but bring us purity and delight. It's going to be good.

"His name will be on their foreheads" (verse 4). I don't think this means we're going to have Jesus' name tattooed on our foreheads, but if that happened, it would be great to wear it. Right now you can't tell the believers from the unbelievers when you're walking down the street, can you? You look much the same as somebody who has absolutely no use for Jesus Christ. But in heaven there will be no doubt that you are a child of God. You will glow. In some way it will be obvious that you are the personal prized possession of Jesus.

John continues, **"There will be no more night. They will not need the light of a lamp or the light of the sun, for the Lord God will give them light"** (verses 5). It'll be like we're back to the first day of creation. Remember that on day one God said, "Let there be light," and there was light? Suddenly the giant mud ball was illuminated. Maybe in about fourth or fifth grade you noticed—hey, wait a minute—the sun didn't get created until day four, so where did the light on day one come from? It was from God! He illuminates everything. Everything is bright and clear around him. The shadows of evil and darkness have no place near him.

Verse 5 goes on to tell us that the Lord God will give us light and that we will reign. Not only do we forgiven sinners get to be close to God and not be afraid. We're also going to be sanctified—we'll be as holy as Christ himself, thanks to what he did for us. Yes, we will reign. It would be an honor above all honors to get to sweep the manure after parades in heaven, if there were some. Man, I would love to have that job in heaven if my alternative is going to hell! Wouldn't you? But we will reign. In other words, we're invited to be part of the management team. WOW! We will reign. We are not only invited to be

> *The Lord God will give us light and we will reign.*

part of the servant core in heaven (which would be sweet in itself), but we will be made kings and priests of the almighty God. Now we are his royalty by faith, but then we will see and know and do his will as princes and princesses of heaven. The angels will serve you and me, and we will serve our God as his royal family.

We **"will reign for ever and ever"** (verse 5). Satan will not torment us ever again. We will look down upon Satan and the demons and say, "You deserve everything you're getting." After all the times that Satan has tormented us and seduced or tricked us into sin, we will finally have power over him, and he will be condemned to what he richly deserves.

Look at verse 6: **"The angel said to me, 'These words are trustworthy and true.'"** "This is all real, John, and it's enough for you now." John's vision was about over. Our virtual tour, our little brochure, our glimpse of heaven has now come to an end. God thinks that this is enough for now. It doesn't begin to answer my questions, but God says to me, "Mark, it's enough for you. Now go and tell other people about my heaven. You don't know everything; you don't know the half of it! But you know enough that you don't have to be afraid of what lies ahead. Instead, rejoice and look forward to it."

As the bodies of your loved ones grow feeble, or as you kneel at someone's bedside holding onto a hand that hardly moves, or when you enter a hospital room to visit someone with a nose full of tubes and a hand with a needle pushed into it, just share some of the comfort and hope of heaven that you have. Don't just talk about the weather or sports when you know someone is dying. Haul out your little virtual tour of heaven!

The amount of time that's left between right now and the time when we will obtain our eternal inheritance is short.

If you know somebody who is depressed and miserable, say, "Hang on, because something great is coming. God has a plan for those who believe in his Son." Whether you have been battered, laid off for eight months, or broken apart by divorce so that you feel you can't trust anybody ever again, trust this: God loves you and has prepared a perfect home for you in heaven. This is trustworthy and true. Satan can't mess with it.

"The Lord, the God of the spirits of the prophets, sent his angel to show his servants the things [on this virtual tour] **that must soon take place"** (verse 6). SOON! Hang on! The amount of time that's left between right now and the time when we will obtain our eternal inheritance is short. Somebody once said that life is like a roll of toilet paper—the closer you get to the end, the faster it goes. Hang on. It won't be long.

The best things are yet to come!

"**Behold,**" says Jesus, "**I am coming soon! Blessed is he who keeps the words of the prophecy in this book**" (verse 7). Yes, Jesus is coming soon to bless us with eternal life. And even now, God is blessing us. He makes good things happen for us as we read and believe what is written in his brochure—his saving Word. And the best things are yet to come!

About the Writer

Pastor Mark Jeske brings the good news of Jesus Christ to viewers of *Time of Grace* in weekly 30-minute programs broadcast across America and around the world on local television, cable, and satellite, as well as on-demand streaming via the Internet. He is the senior pastor at St. Marcus, a thriving multicultural congregation in Milwaukee, Wisconsin. Mark is the author of several books and dozens of devotional booklets on various topics. He and his wife, Carol, have four adult children.

About Time of Grace

Time of Grace is for people who want more growth and less struggle in their spiritual walk. Through the timeless truth of God's Word, we connect people to God's grace so they know they are loved and forgiven and so they can start living in the freedom they've always wanted.

To discover more, please visit timeofgrace.org or call 800.661.3311.

Help share God's message of grace!

Every gift you give helps Time of Grace reach people around the world with the good news of Jesus. Your generosity and prayer support take the gospel of grace to others through our ministry outreach and help them find the restart with Jesus they need.

Give today at timeofgrace.org/give or by calling 800.661.3311.

Thank you!